The Yeshua PRESCRIPTION

Book 1-Self Healing with Christian Healing Oils™

Elyce Monet

BALBOA.
PRESS

A DIVISION OF HAY HOUSE

Balboa Press books may be ordered through booksellers or by contacting:

Balboa Press
A Division of Hay House
1663 Liberty Drive
Bloomington, IN 47403
www.balboapress.com
1 (877) 407-4847

Because of the dynamic nature of the Internet, any web addresses or
links contained in this book may have changed since publication and
may no longer be valid. The views expressed in this work are solely those
of the author and do not necessarily reflect the views of the publisher,
and the publisher hereby disclaims any responsibility for them.

The author of this book does not dispense medical advice or prescribe the use
of any technique as a form of treatment for physical, emotional, or medical
problems without the advice of a physician, either directly or indirectly. The
intent of the author is only to offer information of a general nature to help
you in your quest for emotional and spiritual well-being. In the event you use
any of the information in this book for yourself, which is your constitutional
right, the author and the publisher assume no responsibility for your actions.

Any people depicted in stock imagery provided by Thinkstock are
models, and such images are being used for illustrative purposes only.
Certain stock imagery © Thinkstock.

Print information available on the last page.

ISBN: 978-1-5043-8290-8 (sc)
ISBN: 978-1-5043-8292-2 (hc)
ISBN: 978-1-5043-8291-5 (e)

Library of Congress Control Number: 2017906896

Balboa Press rev. date: 09/25/2017

This book is dedicated to those who are searching for hope and healing.

Don't fear!

You are right where you need to be at this time and God loves you deeply and completely.

> *Is any sick among you? Let him call for the elders of the church; and let them pray over him, anointing him with oil in the name of the Lord: And the prayer of faith shall save the sick, and the Lord shall raise him up; and if he have committed sins, they shall be forgiven him.*
>
> James 5:14-15 (KJV)

Contents

About The Author xi

About the Formulator xiii

Christian Healing Oils... xv

Why This Book 1

Introduction to Healing With Christian Healing Oils™.........7

The History of Healing Oils.. 15

What is Divine Healing? 19

DNA & Ancestral Healing 23

A Medical Perspective 31

Essential Biblical Truths For Healing Yourself 35

Understanding the Steps 39

Doing It! 43

The Power of Relationships... 49

Case Studies As Examples 53

Negative Entities and Dark Spirits.................................. 77

Christian Healing Oils... 81

Anointing Locations 91

Organ Meridian Acupuncture Reflex Points........................ 94

Spinal Chart and Associations 95

Sacred Prayers... 97

Mail-In Coupon 129

About The Author

 **Elyce Monet** is a spiritual healer and wisdom teacher who healed herself after three near-death experiences. She accepted Christ into her heart in her 20s, and has been on a deeply spiritual journey for several decades. She conducts private sessions and workshops to assist people to heal from the inside out.

When she was approached by her friend, Larry Secor, a sacred oils manufacturer and Reiki Master, to write a book about the power of Christian Healing Oils, she was delighted. This book covers healing in a non-traditional way, and yet uses the biblical principles Yeshua used that have been lost through time and misunderstanding.

Elyce has worked in both traditional medicine and natural medicine for more than 20 years, and continues on her quest to help others to heal mind, body and spirit. She says, "Isn't that what we're here for?"

About the Formulator

Larry Secor is a Sacred Healing Oils formulator and manufacturer. Christian Healing Oils™ are completely pure, organic and formulated from the scriptures. Larry is a Reiki Master Healer and wisdom teacher, and teaches workshops on healing. His own journey has included being brought back from the brink of death by God nearly half a dozen times.

For a number of years, he has been creating sacred healing oils and selling them at trade shows and through spiritual healing stores. He asked Elyce to write the manual, knowing they had similar life paths, knew Yeshua intimately as their Lord and Savior, and the desire for all people to heal. It is his heart that all people will be in less pain and understand the power of God to heal through prayer, meditation and anointing.

The Christian Healing Oils™ kit includes 8 Essential Oils (outlined within the book). Each has unique properties for specific healing applications.

At the back of the book is a coupon that can be mailed in for a free sample of an oil of your choice. Elyce and Larry welcome your comments, questions and referrals at http://christianhealingoils.com.

It is our fervent prayer that this healing manual combined with our Christian Healing Oils™ will bring you peace, health and a renewed commitment and faith in the healing power of Jesus Christ.

Why This Book

Never before have I been so pressured by the Holy Spirit to get information to the public. Initially I considered writing this book as a gift of love, but now I see that the prophetic part of this book is much more important than I had considered. In my prayer and meditation, it has been impressed upon me that we are indeed in the end times and the 1st Plague John the Apostle described in Revelation has been unleashed. Think about it. We have "superbugs" that are so powerful that disease is rampant and unstoppable. Cancer is at an all-time high. New diseases are springing up from our polluted water, crops and air. Bioengineering of our food is partly what has created these superbugs, and they appear to be changing our DNA both externally and internally. Wireless technologies are poisoning us and we don't even know it. The radiation that is being emitted by cell phones, towers, microwaves and other devices are frying our brains. We have created a pressure cooker that cannot continue. Additionally, there is conjecture that wireless technologies are interacting with these bioengineered bugs within us, and are beginning to take over our central nervous systems, crossing the blood-brain barrier and creating, in essence, the walking dead. As I worked on this book, Jesus

1

kept taking me to the book of Revelation. It is clear that if we don't heal ourselves, we will not be able to sustain ourselves during the Tribulation. It is upon us like the thief in the night He described.

The information I impart about healing comes from personal experience of near death illnesses, traumas and also by working alongside some of the most brilliant people in their fields, from Nobel-Prize Nominee Research Scientists to Medical and Alternative practitioners and product manufacturers who approach healing with their own unique contribution beyond traditional methodologies. I have also done radio and television with many because of my broadcasting and arts background. I tell you this only to let you know that I was uniquely positioned by God to go through personal health crises in order to share the information I share with you now.

There are three doctors whose practices have been extremely significant in my healing, and I want to give them credit where credit is due. They are Dr. Robert Marshall (Ph.D.) of Premier Research Laboratories, Dr. Vincent Medici, (D.C.) and Dr. Michael Gooing (D.C.). They approach medicine from a mind-body-spirit perspective. Each of them knows Jesus Christ and works on their own spiritual development constantly. I believe they have been guided by Spirit to create new protocols that are ahead of their time. They are affecting health for their patients far beyond traditional understanding. Dr. Marshall created a system for studying the body though nutritional products, energy work and biochemistry. Dr. Medici understood body mechanics, biochemistry and the spirit and soul of the individual. Dr. Gooing has an understanding of epigenetics and brain trauma, and put together frequency medicine and DNA clearing protocols that are unprecedented. I am grateful to all three. Each of them has had a significant impact on my journey of healing, and each of them saved my life in one way or another!

After overcoming 3 major physical traumas that included brain trauma and neurodegeneration, a complete shut-down of the large intestine and growing a tumor the size of a baby, I was called by Spirit to share my experiences with others and became a licensed Christian Spiritual Healer and Certified Life Coach. Since 2011 I have worked with hundreds of people around the world assisting them in their understanding of how to heal themselves spiritually, mentally, emotionally and physically.

My own healing journey has been dramatic. In 1999, after having been diagnosed with 6 months to live, I took an alternative route to healing my body that took me on a significant journey into all aspects of my life. Obviously I didn't die! I opted out of the radical surgery that was recommended by M.D.'s (the removal of my large intestine) and healed myself with the help of Jesus, Dr. Marshall and Dr. Medici. Medical doctors are still scratching their heads over my radical recovery, and the fact that my large intestine, which was completely paralyzed and without function, was functioning normally after 2 years.

After coming back from that near death experience, I suffered a second challenge; a serious fall and significant brain trauma. That was something I didn't expect! I thought I had overcome the worst part, and then suffered an even more serious affliction, experiencing dying and coming back in a matter of seconds. I am still healing myself from the effects of that traumatic brain injury that occurred 12 years ago. What I have come to understand, though, is that the brain injury was a death and rebirth experience that caused me to seek an even deeper journey into spiritual understanding of life and healing. As a result of the brain trauma, I grew a tumor the size of a baby and had to have a hysterectomy, which threw me instantly into menopause before my time. Ouch!

I was never a spiritual slouch. I studied the Bible at seminary level, taught Sunday School and led Bible Studies for 20 years. I started a community non-profit designed to instill spiritual values, and even helped to create a new Christian, Bible-believing, non-denominational church. I wasn't a novice in spiritual practices. I had a very close and intimate relationship with Jesus Christ. My journey after dying and coming back would be with Jesus at the helm, teaching me and guiding me on how to heal myself and eventually others through this book and personal consultations.

This book is written to impart the things I learned through my own healing journey. It is not about changing your faith to heal. My faith in Jesus Christ is still the same. He is my Master Teacher, the Great Healer, and the Son of God. It is only because of Jesus that I am alive and am writing this book. He truly is the Light and Savior of my life. However, through my personal experiences, world travel, and study with master healers from this dimension as well as the spiritual dimensions, I have learned not to judge religious choice. Every path to God the Father is the right path if it brings you closer to Him. We don't choose what religion we are born into. We need to remember that every human being will kneel before Jesus at the appropriate time for them, and that timing is entirely up to God and the individual. As Christians, we need to be admonished that there is a big difference between sharing your love and faith through service and beating someone over the head to believe what you do! Unfortunately, the evangelical training through many churches has taught us to push our opinions and dogma on the world rather than serving through love. We can be assured that acceptance and love will shine through us and provide a natural opportunity to share our faith through service. Remember, it was grace that saved us in Jesus Christ. I admonish my brethren to administer that same grace to others!

I have friends who are Buddhists, Hindus, Jewish, Muslim, Baha'i Faith and more. The only thing that matters is LOVE. Love heals a multitude of sins. I invite all people, regardless of faith, to utilize these practices of Christian Healing Oils™ and the AAA healing system that is explained in the following chapters. Look for the similarities within all faiths, rather than the differences. Remember, we are all descendants through Adam and Eve. That means we are all connected. We are all one in God, no matter what faith, ethnicity, culture or country we were born into. It's now time to begin the journey of acceptance and love rather than separation and hate. It is now time to go beyond our ancestral genetics of fear.

Christian Healing Oils™ is a part of the beginning of your healing journey. I don't believe anything can be the be-all, end-all. It is a start. It can help you get well on your path as you begin your own journey into healing. This is why I selected Christian Healing Oils™ as the beginning step for Christians. It carries God Himself (from His creation of plants) into your tissues and boosts the work you do when you are working on clearing negative thoughts, emotions and ancestral patterns. As you will learn, though, it is not passive healing. You must be ready to commit to making your healing the most important thing in your life. YOU ARE THE AUTHOR OF YOUR HEALTH! You will heal yourself as you learn more about why you are where you are.

My prayer is that you have the commitment to look within and find the beauty and power of who you are in God. You are human and you are a wonderful and remarkable child of God, with God imprinted into every cell of your being! Don't fear! This illness will be used by God to bring you nearer to Him than you have ever been before, if you surrender to it.

2 Corinthians 12:10 - ESV

[10] *For the sake of Christ, then, I am content with weaknesses, insults, hardships, persecutions, and calamities. For when I am weak, then I am strong.*

Introduction to Healing With Christian Healing Oils™

This book is a manual for healing through prayer, meditation and anointing with Christian Healing Oils™. It is designed to provide you with an effective way of healing yourself spiritually, emotionally, mentally and physically. While we do not intend for our sacred Christian Healing Oils™ to take the place of any medical advice or treatment, they can be used practically and safely for healing and as an adjunct therapy, because they rely on all natural ingredients (no toxic ingredients or additives) and the healing power of the vibration (the WORD) of God's voice during creation. Christian Healing Oils™ contain the very essence of God's creation as spoken into being in Genesis.

Gen 1:11, 12 - NIV

¹¹ Then God said, "Let the land produce vegetation: seed-bearing plants and trees on the land that bear fruit with seed in it, according to their various kinds." And it was so. ¹² The land produced vegetation: plants bearing seed according to their kinds and trees bearing fruit with seed in it according to their kinds. And God saw that it was good.

Please note that it is not just the oils that bring healing. Your spiritual, emotional, mental and physical states, as well as your belief systems, habits and patterns, have everything to do with whether or not you heal. Jesus Christ came as a perfect example of how to heal ourselves within the Divine Will of God. He already died on the cross to pay the price for our illness, so that you would have the power to heal yourself. The darkness cannot overtake you if you are diligent and mindful of all aspects of your healing.

As we progress with the healing methodologies in this manual, you may bump up against something that will challenge the way you have thought about yourself, your beliefs, and how you approached healing in the past. Agree to be challenged! If a belief system is ready to be let go, let it go so you can heal! Try all the healing prayers and meditations contained in this book. When I was near death, I decided that I was willing to do anything to heal, even if it meant having to stand on my head naked in the corner! While that seems like a silly statement, that is how surrendered to God we need to be when it comes to healing. I felt no shame or condemnation over trying it all, and I wasn't worried about what anybody else thought. I was simply on a mission to learn what had caused me my illness and how I could change it so I could heal. I stood before God naked, with nothing to hide. Healing is all about transparency before Him.

I knew that my time of service here on planet Earth was not complete, so I needed to do my due diligence to find out what I had done to cause this and how I could heal myself. Remember,

God uses all things in our lives to get us to reach for Him, even illness and disease. In many ways, the things that are the most difficult are actually meant for our good; as opportunities for us to grow and evolve as spiritual beings. Even the great Apostle Paul had some kind of torment that was his "thorn in the flesh" that God did not take away. God allowed it to stay. Whether or not this was illness nobody knows. We just know that there are some things that are there for God's good reason.

2 Cor 12:7 - KJV2000

And lest I should be exalted above measure through the abundance of these revelations, there was given to me a thorn in the flesh, a messenger of Satan to torment me.

We can learn much about ourselves if we are willing to open our eyes, ears and hearts and be willing to face the truth. Even the great Apostle Paul suffered and God allowed it!

I found in my ongoing pursuit for healing that belief systems are the primary key to whether or not we heal. What is a belief system? It is simply something we think and feel repetitively until it becomes embodied, and we act on it subconsciously as truth. Most times, these are old belief systems we took on from the conditioning of our parents and authority figures while growing up and the feelings surrounding them. We need to examine them for truth and let them go if they no longer resonate with where we are. Let me give you an example of a very prominent belief system that gets in the way of our healing.

We have been conditioned to believe that healing is external. Often, when we get sick, we take a pill or have something (like an organ) cut out. The problem with that kind of belief system is that it never addresses the underlying cause of the illness; it simply cuts out the organ. How many other organs will be affected if we don't get to the root of the problem? Traditional medical doctors have unfortunately been trained in this belief system. Most times they treat symptoms rather than identifying the source of the manifestation of illness in the body.

In order to look deeper into the causes of dis-ease in the body, it takes an open heart to hear and try new therapies, whether they are covered by insurance or not! As I have worked with many, I have found that often the limiting belief has been around money. "I can't afford it" is often the most common block to healing. While our society has been conditioned to go to doctors and hospitals that cost thousands of dollars, it is easy to set up that mental block. The truth, however, is that you can make great strides in your health by changing that belief system and opening up to the infinite supply of abundance in God. I remember in my own life saying I could never afford my healing. My doctor at the time reminded me that if I put myself first and let God supply what I needed, I would create an environment for myself that was conducive to my healing and money wouldn't be a problem. That year I worked half as hard and tripled my income. My expenses were covered. I began to see that I had the power to co-create my life the way I wanted it to be, and that included money and health.

Because our minds and belief systems are so powerful,

we are very often completely unaware of what we are doing that is not in alignment with Universal Truth (God) until it's too late and illness manifests. That's when we need to accept that we have been asleep at the wheel. But don't despair! You got yourself into this, and you can get yourself out! It will take perseverance and patience, but you can do it!

It is believed by many doctors now that the real reason we get sick is because we are repeatedly experiencing traumas on many different levels that are repressed and ignored. This is all caused by our lack of understanding and awareness. It is easy for us to see "stress" as a trigger and a cause, but how do we pinpoint what "stress" is? How do we understand the differences between mental stress, emotional stress, environmental stress, ancestral stress, physical stress, etc.? It is high time we get to the roots of illness so they can be cleansed once and for all, rather than going to a doctor for treatment of symptoms. We need to learn that all healing happens within us on a cellular level. When you allow God to work with your open mind and heart, beyond the limits of human belief systems, miracles can happen within your cells!

We also need to learn to be patient with ourselves. We didn't get sick overnight. Serious illness happens over many years. Your physical body is the last place the sickness is manifested. So don't expect to heal everything instantly. It is like peeling the layers of an onion. It takes work. It can make you cry. It takes insight. It takes surrender like you've never surrendered before, layer by layer. Through the journey, however, you will find out many beautiful things about yourself. You will learn how precious you are to God, and the power within you to change your life for the better. God uses everything in our lives, including illness, to help us come to terms with how much we are loved and how powerful we are.

I also personally recommend ALL HEALING MODALITIES, so as not to limit healing. Our bodies are very complicated, and can and should be treated simultaneously medically, holistically, and spiritually. This manual is a guide to help you heal traumas primarily from a spiritual perspective (because it involves mind-body-spirit), but we do not believe that Christian Healing Oils™ and spiritual practices are the ONLY way to heal. If you are sick, get help from all sources you trust. I traveled the world working on my health with many Masters in Eastern Medicine as well as working with traditional Medical Doctors and Natural Holistic Practitioners. They all have a place in our healing, as do prescription drugs. If I have an infection in my body, it is prudent to get an antibiotic to clear the infection. If I have a broken leg, I want a medical doctor to reset it, not a spiritual healer (although I reset my own broken hand beautifully with faith without knowing it was broken)! I personally utilize as many holistic practices as possible, because I believe the more natural the better. However, use your own inner guidance to guide you to what feels right and wrong. You are the one in the driver's seat of your ongoing healing, not any doctor, healer, family member or friend. You know your body and soul better than anyone except God. Go within yourself to ask God what your steps are to co-create great health. You might be surprised. You may get guidance to go to a therapist that can help you heal your emotional wounds. You might be guided to get acupuncture to release stuck energy. You might be guided to exercise and diet. You might be guided to get significant blood panels to discover bacteria and viruses that may be in your body. And you might be guided to work on ancestral genetic issues lying dormant in your DNA. It is all done in stages. We all have more than just the physical body. We are multi-dimensional beings, and for healing to work, we need to work on all the subtle bodies (emotional, mental, etc.) as well as the physical. Let God guide you step by step. Listen to everyone, and make your decisions in your prayer closet, alone with God. When your heart is flooded with peace, you will know you are on the right path.

The History of Healing Oils

Sacred healing oils have been used in healing practices and ceremonies for thousands of years, and are still prominent today as non-toxic, medicinal remedies. Our oils have been extracted from plant essences and formulated from both Biblical references and the study of the teachings of Jesus Christ and the Essenes, the healing group from which we believe Him to have belonged and practiced.

The Essenes were the healers of their time. Dr. Edmond Bordeaux Szekely, a principal translator of Essene materials before the discovery of the Dead Sea Scrolls, describes the Essene Community:

> *"They spent much time in study, both of ancient writings and special branches of learning, such as education, healing and astronomy. ......In the use of plants and herbs for healing man and beast they were likewise proficient.*
>
> *They lived a simple regular life, rising each day before sunrise to study and commune with the forces of nature, bathing in cold water as a ritual and donning white garments. After their daily labor in the fields and vineyards they partook of their meals in silence, preceding and ending it with prayer. They*

were entirely vegetarian in their eating and never touched flesh foods nor fermented liquids. Their evenings were devoted to study and communion with the heavenly forces. ...

Their way of life enabled them to live to advanced ages of 120 years or more and they were said to have marvelous strength and endurance. In all their activities they expressed creative love."

This manual is designed to provide you with simple first steps to learn the same healing methods Jesus Christ practiced while he was on Earth. You have everything you need within you to open your heart and heal yourself, as long as you are within God's will. The oils, prayers and sacred ceremonies are simply suggestions and tools for connecting you to Christ, His holy angels, and other enlightened Masters. Your work, which will be outlined in this manual, will be to learn how to receive the Divine Essences and the emanations of the Holy Spirit and the living vibration of Creator God contained in your Christian Healing Oils. Healing is an ongoing process which requires minute by minute self-examination, prayer, meditation and action. We are exhorted to take every thought captive for the uplifting of all. It is this mental/emotional process that provides you with many secrets to healing yourself.

2 Cor 10:5- ASV

Casting down imaginations, and every high thing that is exalted against the knowledge of God, and bringing every thought into captivity to the obedience of Christ.

Please note that healing always starts with YOU. Once you have become clear in your abilities to feel and receive Divine Love and healing, and have seen success in your own self practice, then and only then should you attempt to heal another. Manual #2 will take you deeper into self-healing and provide you with beginning models for healing others.

We at Christian Healing Oils™ send you divine blessings and love on your journey of healing. Remember, even when life seems difficult, He is always working on our behalf.

Rom 8:28 - NASB

And we know that all things work together for good to them that love God, to them who are the called according to his purpose.

What is Divine Healing?

In order to begin to heal, we need to become aware that something within us (our mind, our emotions, our human will and/or our body) is out of synch with Divinity and needs to be recalibrated. Many times we turn to God when we get sick or someone we love is struggling with health issues. This is a natural and commendable thing to do. It shows that we know deeply somehow that we are connected to God and need healing for ourselves and others that is beyond our ability.

So let's start at the beginning. As human beings, we are born in a binary system. Some call it duality – with both human and divine natures. But it wasn't always that way. In Genesis, we see that we were once in a physically, emotionally and spiritually perfect God-state, made in God's image.

Genesis 1:27 - NIV

So God created mankind in his own image, in the image of God he created them; male and female He created them.

What this means is that being created like God (Father, Son & Holy Spirit) was our ORIGINAL state (in a triune system), and God's light was contained in every cell in our bodies in

19

perfect health. We were exceptional God-like beings that were given the free will to love God and obey His commands. But then…. Oops. We blew it! We didn't choose God. You know the story. Eve was deceived by the serpent, showed Adam, and together they disobeyed. Instead of physical death, humankind suffered a spiritual death. The light of God that I spoke of before that existed in every cell within our bodies went out like a switch was turned off. I believe this is the shutting off (forgetting) our God DNA until we really reach back for Him! I discuss that more in the next chapter on DNA and Ancestral Healing. It is critical to understand that all disease entered the world because we are now in a Human DNA state rather than a God DNA state. Until our DNA is turned back on to God, we can't heal ourselves. We will remain in a state of fallen human genetics without the most important component-God! When we are in dis-ease in the body, it is essential that we go to our divine source (God) for healing so that we can be operating by our Divine DNA or God Blueprint within us. We need to bring the "As Above" (God) to the "So Below" (Man). That is the Divine illumination into the human body, or the God-Mind.

It is also very important to remember that both masculine and feminine sides of our natures need to be examined and healed. For example, look at how our brains function. The left side of the brain (masculine) is all about wisdom, thoughts, action, logic and processes. The right side of the brain (feminine) is all about understanding, intuition, feeling, creativity and bringing energy into physical form (manifestation). Just as the man creates life through the wisdom of the sperm, so does the woman nurture life within herself, in order to bring understanding and compassion into physical form. It is God's design of creation that we need each other and have both masculine and feminine within ourselves.

In the healing process, it will be necessary to explore our thoughts, feelings, actions, past and reactions in order to become more aware of where we are out of synch with God's Divine Blueprint. Understanding the body as being more than just physical is necessary in order to heal. As we open our hearts to Divine Healing of mind-body-spirit, we open our genetic keys to higher vibrational light codes that trigger a chemical process in our cells to bring healing.

DNA & Ancestral Healing

We are all connected to God and to each other through our DNA. Until we understand that each of us is connected to everyone and everything God created, we will not be able to go beyond our ancestral wounding, and that includes the genetics of diseased states. That's why we are born with predispositions to disease.

I find it very intriguing that for years scientists said that we had two stranded DNA and lots of useless "junk" DNA. That junk DNA carries a lot more than we knew! They have since retracted their statements about our disorganized DNA being "junk". In fact, they now believe it may hold within it the decoding of the evolution of our species. They also retracted their belief that DNA was set in stone. It is now scientifically proven that we can change our DNA. That's good news! That means that any negative genetic patterns that we inherited through DNA from our ancestors can be overcome.

Many believe that this junk DNA is being reorganized into a third strand of DNA through the chemical mutative process of our cells. Think about it. Then, instead of operating on a dualistic or binary system, we would operate as a trinity. And does it make sense that our DNA may once have been a 3 stranded helix before the fall? Or just maybe there were more than 3? Is it something we can reclaim? Perhaps as a civilization we need to mutate a few more thousand years. However, we are beginning to see this new DNA become part of our reality. There is documentation about at least one child born with 3 strands of DNA. Scientists are also finding that our DNA is mutating as a species, and we are capable of 12 full strands of DNA. Check out the following link for the facts.

http://myscienceacademy.org/2013/01/23/scientists-finally-present-evidence-on-expanding-dna-strands/

The important thing to deal with now is the fact that something in our DNA has been lying dormant. I'm going to call this "human DNA", and I am going to call our turned on spiritually DNA "God DNA". No, we don't have separate sets of DNA; we simply forgot our connection to God! That has brought us much pain and suffering, all which is based in fear. It takes a remembering, an "awakening" or "enlivening" of our DNA in order to be connected to God and heal ourselves. This is not a one-time profession of faith in church. This goes much deeper and is connected to spiritual growth as the precursor to good health in a biological sense.

Once our DNA becomes activated in our "Divine" state, we have within us the power to heal ourselves. Without it, there is only what mankind has created and determined from the human mind. The human mind is simply a computer that processes garbage in-garbage out and forms decisions based on experience. The problem is that healing without God is like trying to mend a tear in a box by using the same methods that created the tear! Conversely, when we allow the light (God) to enliven our DNA, we have the same abilities to heal as did Jesus. Miracles happen!

We must REMEMBER and ACT UPON Divine Truth within us in order to release our fallen state and return to our original God-DNA. This is the same act of making the decision to accept Christ into our hearts, but it is done second by second as we become more aware of our God DNA, which is sometimes called the "higher self".

Our higher spiritual truths are manifest through a process of each individual's own unique journey of awareness, transformation and transmutation. We are exhorted biblically to be transformed by the renewing of our minds on a minute by minute basis. We are saved by grace, minute by minute! It is NOT a one-time profession of faith that gives us the ability to heal ourselves. That is simply the beginning of the journey. Once reborn in Spirit, we share in His sufferings, and it is through our sufferings that the opportunities for true magical transformation are revealed.

Rom 12:2 - NIV

Do not conform to the pattern of this world, but be transformed by the renewing of your mind. Then you will be able to test and approve what God's will is— his good, pleasing and perfect will.

Let's talk about your first decision to accept Christ into our hearts. Primarily in the Christian Churches, this is a mental decision based on the prompting of the Holy Spirit in our hearts that we need to make the decision, and we make it. The making the decision is the mental decision of choice. This is great, and is the first step to healing our core wound with God of separation. The problem is that we think that's all there is to it! It's not. We must take action minute by minute to go into our hearts and make mental decisions from there. If we simply choose to walk the aisle for Christ and make a profession of faith, we will fall flat. The heart is the only thing God cares about! And we can't continue in growth until we embody this truth with heart and mind. It takes both, and I like to call it the Heart-Mind. Did you know that the heart has its own mind? Look at the Heart Math Center online and see all the research about the power of the heart. Scientific evidence suggests that the heart is FAR MORE POWERFUL than the mind alone.

I am assuming that as a Christian reading this book, you have already accepted Christ into your heart. If not, then consider this an invitation into a journey into knowing Him. It is not about a profession of faith or standing in front of a congregation professing your faith. It is about your state of heart, and your desire to truly know God.

If you are a non-Christian and are trained in the ways of enlightened beings other than Jesus Christ, then this manual also applies to your healing with an invitation to meet Jesus Christ, the Great Healer. Perhaps through using these protocols, you will come to know Him in addition to the enlightened one you may be working with. Jesus and Christianity (the church) are not exclusive. They are (or rather, should be) inclusive.

Jesus spoke and healed the woman at the well (a Samaritan) who didn't know Him. He can heal anyone where they are, as long as they open their hearts. Christians who get caught up in dogma of "we are the only answer" are missing the point! Don't let Christians with judgment and ego stop you from learning about Jesus. Each and every person comes to know God through Divine Grace. It is a free gift, and Christians need to be mindful that God has His timing for that Grace to be delivered to each and every soul. We are not to judge but to uplift, knowing that we are responsible only for sharing love and the opportunity for God's grace. We are not responsible for a person's awakening, healing or salvation.

Eph 2:8,9 - NIV

For it is by grace you have been saved, through faith- -and this is not from yourselves, it is the gift of God- not by works, so that no one can boast....

If you accepted Christ in a church, revival meeting, or bible study, and did not follow through with learning more about your experience, you may have questioned the magic of it. It is time to get back on track. This manual will help you continue the journey, take responsibility for your circumstances, and begin to investigate your opportunities to snuggle up to God, the Source of all healing.

Getting to know Christ, God's Son, the perfect man, is an ongoing process, not a one-time thing. Jesus lived a completely human life here on Earth and provided us with all the information we need to go into higher consciousness by enlivening our DNA. It is through His conquering death that we have the power to heal. So examine yourself and be honest about where you are.

This guide will help you become aware of the truth of who you really are in God through prayer and meditation, and then guide you through the steps needed to activate your God-DNA so you can heal on all levels. When we do these steps, a chemical reaction happens within our Human-DNA and genetic codes are chemically turned on to enable us to receive light. It is as if the shadows surrounding our DNA strands are unwound by this light. So what is light? Light is what is described in the Bible as God Himself!

1 John 1:5 – NIV

This is the message we have heard from him and declare to you: God is light; in Him there is no darkness at all.

As we begin to heal, it is not only a biological process, but a spiritual one that is encoded in the very fabric of our existence as humans.

So what are some of the most important Divine Truths of healing?

I am not separated from God, even when I feel like I am.

Rom 8:38,39 - NASB

And I am convinced that nothing can ever separate us from God's love. Neither death nor life, neither angels nor demons, neither our fears for today nor our worries about tomorrow—not even the powers of hell can separate us from God's love.

<u>I am capable of handling anything that comes into my reality through the power of God.</u>

Phil 4:13 - NASB

"I can do all things through Him who strengthens me."

A Medical Perspective

Many scientists, holistic practitioners and medical doctors now believe and understand that trauma is what creates all illness and dis-ease in the body, and it can happen at many levels; physical, emotional, psychological, environmental, spiritual, and semantic (which includes ancestral). These traumas are also cumulative; they remain in the body until they are cleared. Thousands of books have been written on the subject, mainly by those physicians who have gone deeply into healing on a DNA level. We invite you to check out the works of Richard Gerber, M.D., Bruce Lipton, Ph.D. (Biology of Belief), Gregg Braden (Spontaneous Healing of Belief), Christian Fleche, (Biodecoding), Patrick Obissier, Keith Scott-Mumby, MD., Ph.D., etc. just to name a few.

Traumas happen every day, beginning in the womb and continuing throughout our lives. Trauma can be a biological organism (flu, cold, illness, etc.) a physical injury, an environmental incident (toxic air, radiation, electromagnetic interference, etc.), emotional pain that wounded us, and more. When the body has traumas it can't correct it will automatically compensate and adapt. Over time, this compromises our immune system, and our body gets sick from the toxic overload.

31

Getting well does not necessarily mean you have cleared the trauma; it simply means your body stores it in an organ somewhere so you can continue to function. Once the body can no longer compensate and adapt you will become symptomatic and an illness will express itself. Our goal is to go to the root issue of the illness and let Christ cleanse it completely on a cellular level so that the illness doesn't return.

We are all electrical beings. It is now agreed upon in the traditional medical field that our bio field (auric field) is electric. So much for the "woo woo" aura readers! They had it right all the time! I guess they had to be the ones to bring it forth and be laughed at for decades before the traditional societies could accept it as truth. Now the auric field or electrical bio field, as it is called in medical circles, is part of the medical system. You might be interested to know that most everything in the body is electric! Even the chemical processes in the body take electricity to create the chemical reaction. The medical community at large has been treating the biochemical aspects of the body and has largely ignored the electrical until recently, with some exceptions.

Because traumas are electrical frequencies, they operate on frequency levels, and can alter our DNA. Think in terms of polarities and magnets. One magnet attracts in another magnet and they stick together and become one. The truth is that is exactly what we do. We have a trauma, and it acts like a magnet and connects with the frequency we carry in our DNA code. I personally struggled with this until I understood it may or may not be something I am DOING. It may just be happening because it is in my ancestral DNA. You see, we also carry our ancestors' traumas through our DNA. This is what is meant in the bible by "the iniquities of the fathers are visited upon the children". It is through our DNA!

Another thing scientists have learned about DNA is that it is constantly interacting with our mind, will and emotions, as well as our external or environmental conditions, as written in articles by Grazyna Fosar and Franz Bluudorf. Here are excerpts:

> *"THE HUMAN DNA IS A BIOLOGICAL INTERNET and superior in many aspects to the artificial one. There is evidence for a whole new type of medicine in which DNA can be influenced and reprogrammed by words and frequencies WITHOUT cutting out and replacing single genes.*
>
> *Only 10% of our DNA is being used for building proteins. It is this subset of DNA that is of interest to western researchers and is being examined and categorized. The other 90% are considered "junk DNA." The Russian researchers, however, convinced that nature was not dumb, joined linguists and geneticists in a venture to explore those 90% of "junk DNA."*
>
> *Their results, findings and conclusions are simply revolutionary! According to them, our DNA is not only responsible for the construction of our body but also serves as data storage and in communication. The Russian linguists found that the genetic code, especially in the apparently useless 90%, follows the same rules as all our human languages. To this end they compared the rules of syntax (the way in*

which words are put together to form phrases and sentences), semantics (the study of meaning in language forms) and the basic rules of grammar. The Russian biophysicist and molecular biologist Pjotr Garjajev and his colleagues also explored the vibrational behavior of the DNA. The bottom line was: "Living chromosomes function just like solitonic/ holographic computers using the endogenous DNA laser radiation."

"This means that they managed for example to modulate certain frequency patterns onto a laser ray and with it influenced the DNA frequency and thus the genetic information itself. One can simply use words and sentences of the human language! This, too, was experimentally proven! Living DNA substance (in living tissue, not in vitro) will always react to language-modulated laser rays and even to radio waves, if the proper frequencies are being used."

What science found in deep human biological study was something Christ and the Essenes already knew and practiced! We can change our DNA and our bodies at all levels through prayer, meditation, confession, plants (healing oils) and by changing our thoughts and emotional patterns by reaching for God. I call it Sacred or Divine Healing. Funny that it has taken us more than 2000 years to discover something that was accepted and practiced so long ago. It just goes to prove that when we are operating in our human blueprint, we are a little slow!

Essential Biblical Truths
For Healing Yourself

Have you ever noticed that when you put your mind and heart to something, you can usually accomplish it? That's because **WHERE YOU FOCUS YOUR MIND AND HEART IS WHAT YOU CREATE/ MANIFEST.**

So what is focus? You will hear the word "consciousness" a lot. I used to be a little confused by that word, not understanding what it meant, until I learned that it is the same thing as where I put the attention of my mind and heart - FOCUS. Our FOCUS is our conscious mind using its God-given power to create. Everything in your world is and has been created by you, either with or without God, by design or by default. It is high time we begin to understand the truth of the power within us. We are creating our reality whether we know it or not, with every thought, with every emotion, and with every action. If you want to see what your belief system is, look around you at your creation! The way you live, the way you spend your money, the people in your life and your relationship to them, your work, your choices, all reflect your belief system and where you have FOCUSED or NOT FOCUSED your energy. That's right... when you are in an UN-FOCUSED state, you are still creating...

from your *subconscious*. Your outer world is a reflection of all the choices you made from your inner belief system, and many times you are creating without consciously being aware of it. When the subconscious mind is in control without the FOCUSED GUIDANCE of the conscious mind, we repeat old habits, patterns and traumas. Funny thing is that we can't figure out why we keep getting the same negative result! It's because we are allowing our subconscious habits and patterns to create our reality. Conscious co-creation of the life we want starts with taking responsibility for ourselves and understanding and believing in the power we truly have. It is God's Gift!

Many people deny responsibility for illness and negative circumstances, blaming others… even God! It's time to change. We can't heal if we don't take responsibility! God didn't make you sick… you made you sick from years of bad habits and patterns. Most times, God didn't afflict you. In fact, even in the book of Job, it states that God allowed Satan to buffet Job. God didn't afflict him. Satan did. But God allowed it. Sometimes that is what it takes to become aware of our values and choices in life. Many times, you have made choices based on what you were conditioned to believe, and you were not acting out of your higher self or Divine blueprint. It's o.k. We all do it. Once you take responsibility for having created your situation or illness, you can confess it, cleanse it, and bring compassion to yourself. Forgiving yourself for what you didn't know is all part of the process. We aren't meant to focus on our mistakes, (when we focus there we create more mistakes!) but rather on the *truth of who we really are and where we want to be.*

Christ gave us the keys to consciously co-create our life WITH GOD, rather than allowing our subconscious habits and patterns to carry us along in the drift of life. He was our perfect example of how to do it, by focusing His mind on the things of God rather than the things of this world. When we do that, we can co-create a divine existence that heals every aspect of our lives. But it takes work! We must be consciously aware of what we are doing and change it!

Rom 12:2 - NIV

Do not conform to the pattern of this world, but be transformed by the renewing of your mind. Then you will be able to test and approve what God's will is— his good, pleasing and perfect will.

1st John gives us the prescription for healing ourselves. It includes awareness of our human state (sin) and what we must do to heal and receive God's light.

1John 1:5-10 - NIV

"And this is the message we have heard from Him and announced to you that God is light and in Him there is no darkness at all. If we say that we have fellowship with Him and yet walk in the darkness, we lie and do not practice the truth. But if we walk in the light as He Himself is in the light, we have fellowship with one another and the blood of Jesus, His Son, cleanses us from all sin. If we say that we have no sin, we are deceiving ourselves and the truth is not in us. If we

confess our sins, He is faithful and righteous to forgive us our sins and to cleanse us from all unrighteousness."

The prescription for our darkness (illness) is simple.

1) Become **AWARE** of our need for God by examining our thoughts, emotions and environments in which we find ourselves. (Hearing the Still, Small Voice of God within)
2) **AWAKEN** to the truth of what needs to be changed in our lives. (Believing the Still, Small Voice of God within as TRUTH so we can take personal responsibility for ourselves)
3) Take **ACTION to** purify ourselves, which is the act of confessing and forsaking whatever is out of alignment with God's will.

Once we activate our divine blueprint within (awaken to our God-DNA by confessing and releasing our "shadow" pattern of victim consciousness that feels separate from God) then we are cleansed by light and the healing begins.

Our perfect example is Jesus, of course, who gave us many examples of healing. He healed lepers, those paralyzed, a woman hemorrhaging, the blind, the lame, those oppressed by demons, and even raising people from the dead. They are recorded in the Gospels and are easy to find. But he also taught the disciples, who also began healing themselves and others. You can do the same thing today. It's biblical and Godly!

Understanding the Steps

So now that you are ready to heal, I want to share 3 stages in the healing process already revealed in the last chapter.

PHASE 1: AWARENESS (The voice of who we are being)

PHASE 2: AWAKENING (The belief and responsibility of who we are being)

PHASE 3: ACTION (Creating conscious actions based on truth to affect a positive outcome)

So let's define what each of these phases is about.

Phase 1: AWARENESS

The first phase of healing requires understanding that I have both a conscious and subconscious mind. The conscious mind is like the captain of the ship giving orders, and the subconscious mind is the engine crew that actually does the work from below deck that no one sees. The crew (your subconscious mind) is always there and is always working. It is aware of memories, emotions and traumas that are available to recall. It is also in constant contact with your unconscious mind, which is the part of our consciousness we can't recall by ourselves. So for the purpose of healing with Christian Oils, let's discuss and work with the conscious and subconscious minds.

The best way to become aware is to enter into a state of prayer and meditation and ask God's help for the truth to probing questions about why we are experiencing this and that. Then we need to listen for our heart's answer. That is NOT the negative voice inside your head telling you nasty things about yourself. That is from the pit of hell. Ignore it. The answers I am talking about come from your heart, and tell you that you are loved and nothing can separate you from the love of God. It offers gentle and loving guidance into the truth of our shadow side or human mistakes.

Phase 2: AWAKENING

The second phase of healing involves accepting the truth about who we are BEING. It is important to note that we are called human beings, not human doings. We have been so conditioned by the world to think that who we are is based on what we do. However, the truth is that our lives are created by our thoughts and emotions, followed by our actions. If we want to change and heal ourselves, we start with who we are BEING. What we think, how we feel, what charges us into action both positively and negatively. The still, small voice within us has given us information about ourselves. Now we have to ask, "Is it truth?" This is the phase that takes much courage, and becomes the activator of our God DNA. If we are willing to face ourselves, and surrender our will to God's will, then the awakening and grace will pour into us and enliven every cell within our bodies with light. We will be given divine power to change anything we need to change within ourselves. But Jesus said this:

Matt 26:41- NIV

"Watch and pray so that you will not fall into temptation. The spirit is willing, but the flesh is weak."

We must have the courage to admit to ourselves the truth and come out of denial. If we don't, there will be no healing. If we do, we are unstoppable, capable of changing our lives in every way we desire!

Some people have been so closed off from their inner voice that they have trouble hearing the truth in their heart. There are several ways to address this: 1) Continue on in prayer, asking for God's grace to hear the truth 2) Get a Spiritual Coach who can assist you in understanding what Spirit is saying and assist you to move at a pace that is comfortable for you. Having a guide is sometimes very helpful, since we are all somewhat blinded to our own shadow side. It helps to have an objective, trained coach or pastor who can give you assistance. I have done this work for years and work with other Spiritual Healers whom you can interview. Simply write me at info@ christianhealingoils.com for information.

Phase 3: ACTION

The third phase is ONGOING ACTION. Once you are committed to awakening, you must take steps toward God. These involve prayer and meditation, confession and then ongoing obedience to follow what you are told. It sounds so simple, yet we make it so complicated! The action steps must be repeated and embodied if we are to change our lives. Step by step instructions follow in the next chapter.

Action also involves visualization, a technique that has been used for thousands of years to "see" God at work. It is not done with your physical eyes, but rather with your eyes closed and through the imagination. Visualization helps us to see ourselves as healed, and to feel the effects of that healing in our bodies. It also sets up the mind to positively accept the healing and believe it to be truth. If the mind does not believe it, the healing will not take place. It is important to visualize ourselves as we want to be in order to co-create our new, healthy state.

Doing It!

STEPS TO PHASE 1 – AWARENESS

Find A Quiet Place. Sit in a comfortable chair with your feet firmly planted on the floor and your palms up in your lap. (Attitude of surrender) A quiet, undistracted environment is necessary to go deep within.

Anoint yourself with Christian Healing Oils* and Pray. *Oils could be Three Kings for Opening yourself to God, and Mary Magdalene for deep meditation. Consult the Chapter about Application of Christian Healing Oils for more information. Pray and ask for truth! You may use the prayers in the back of this book as guidelines.

Next, ask God to give you the truth from your heart on the answers to these questions:

> **Where has my focus been on this issue? (ON MYSELF, ON OTHERS)**
>
> Am I being selfish or do I lack boundaries for myself?
>
> Am I operating consciously or subconsciously?
>
> **Who am I being? (VICTIM, JUDGE, RESCUER)**

43

It is important to understand that we all play all three, although we have a default to one of them most of the time. When we are able to see ourselves in each role, we can clear the negative habits and patterns. Here are some descriptions of each role:

Victim – I see others (and/or God) as hurting me. I am in self-pity. Negative emotion attached is usually sadness, depression, anxiety.

Judge – I see others (and/or God) as hurting me and make them bad and wrong for what they are doing. Negative emotion attached is usually frustration, anger, rage, indignance or intolerance.

Rescuer – Others (and/or God) can't do things without me. Negative emotion attached is usually seen as interference, control, over nurturing and overly sympathetic.

What is my belief system around this issue? (Is there an old belief system that is ready to be acknowledged and changed?)

Remember when I said your STATE OF BEING has everything to do with your healing? By becoming aware of where my focus is and who I am being I can begin to discover the hidden belief system that is buried in my subconscious and is causing me misalignment with my Divine Blueprint.

STEPS IN PHASE 2: AWAKENING

Listen to the messages that come through about who you are being.

Feel it DEEPLY and own it.

Feel the pain of being separate from God in this place.

Ask yourself, "Am I ready to surrender to change?"

> Awakening to God is about facing our own demons and traumas head on. If we aren't willing to look and accept them as being real, we can't heal. It is all about owning the truth of our own darkness, and having compassion for ourselves that all humans have this need to face themselves where they deny God. Most times, we have only done it out of fear.
>
> Focus on your desire to change, having compassion for yourself. We all fall short as humans, and there must be a healthy balance between deeply knowing the pain we have created in ourselves and others and forgiving ourselves for it.

Awakening is the part that takes the most courage. Awakening is a soul choice. If you don't accept the awareness deep into your heart as truth you will not be able to effect change. You can even take drastic measures externally, but it won't work with God. God cannot be manipulated. He knows if your heart is true. If it is not, you will continue to recycle old habits and patterns until you come to the end of yourself! So be mindful of the opportunities we have to awaken. Hold them as precious. You are being called by God in this place of your life. Listen. Face your demons (literally and metaphorically), and then take action toward change. It isn't about perfection; it is about the willingness of your soul and asking for God's help.

STEPS IN PHASE 3: ACTION

Anoint yourself with Christian Healing Oils*

See Chapters on Application of Christian Healing Oils

Pray a Prayer of Confession

See Chapter on Specific Prayers you can use and adapt, or just pray to Father God from your heart.

*Note that I make the distinction of praying to the Father, because we were directed by Jesus to pray to the Father, not to Jesus directly.

Matt 6:6 - NIV

But when you pray, go into your room, close the door and pray to your Father, who is unseen. Then your Father, who sees what is done in secret, will reward you.

Ask God what Action you need to take to create this new way of being.

Your initial request may bring forth one or two steps you are to take immediately.

Thereafter, you need to repeat anointing and praying daily in order to walk in newness of life. If we don't ask for daily help, we will simply fall back into old patterns.

Modern psychology has determined that it takes 21 days for a new practice to become a habit (or embodied into our subconscious). We must consider our old habit as rendered powerless, although the mind loop will still be running. We cannot erase a mind loop. We can only create a new one. *So for a minimum of 21 days, anointing, prayer, meditation and action are needed to create total change in your life.*

The Power of Relationships

One thing I have come to know intimately is that relationships are where we truly reveal ourselves for who we are being in any given moment. This means that every relationship in your life has the power to transform your illness.

You have heard about The Law of Attraction. This is simply a modern version of a Universal Truth of how we are designed; our inside life is reflected in our outside life so that we can see who we are being. What I have learned is that who we are being (from our subconscious mind) may be exhibited rather than what we want to be exhibited. This is often the case.

We are so programmed and conditioned that we are on auto-pilot. We need to become more and more aware of what we are saying, what we are thinking and what we are doing. It all starts with awareness and the vulnerability that says, "I don't know it all. I can open my mind to hear your heart and what you are saying behind your words. I am willing to be wrong. I am willing to learn something new about myself and about you."

Our lifetime is all about learning who we truly are. God has designed us so that we attract in the same frequency at which we are vibrating, or we attract in the frequency that is the opposite of what we are vibrating so that we can mirror back to ourselves our own pattern.

In my life, the most important mirrors were my relationships, and I have come to learn that this is truth for all. It begins with our relationship to God and extends to our primary intimate relationships (husband/wife), then to our children, our coworkers and friends, and so on.

The victim pattern for me was a significant one. I kept attracting more and more abusers until I figured out that I was playing the victim! Once I owned the victim-ness of my own thoughts, I was able to go beyond playing the role and the abuse stopped. Most people will find themselves in one of the roles most comfortably. Since the victim state is the state of non-self –responsibility, it is the one most of us are utilizing.

How we treat those we are closest to is usually the most telling of where we need to do healing work on ourselves. Don't worry. Everyone is this way and you are not unique. It is simply God's design to help us to see ourselves in the mirrors of those closest to us so that we can begin to accept where we are out of alignment. What it means, though, is that it is time to put down your pride and defensiveness. God already sees your pride and arrogance. It is no secret to Him! It is you who is hiding from yourself.

Relationships are the most important part of life. When you think about it, everything is about relationship. How I relate to my partner. How I relate to my kids. How I relate to my siblings. How I relate to my customers in business. How I relate to government. How I relate to my dog. How I relate to nature. How I relate to people who disagree with me. How I relate to those of different color and belief systems. Everything in life is a virtual learning ground when it comes to relationships. It is the most complex place for awakening, and so God uses it to help us find truth and light.

I exhort you to look at your relationships first. Where are you being dogmatic? Where are you insisting that you are right and others wrong?

What are other people saying to you? In my own awakening process, one of my children told me that I was the one of the most judgmental people she had ever known. That hurt my heart so badly, I went straight to God! And I learned she was right! Many years ago, I had adopted a pattern of right and wrong, good and bad, and had forgotten compassion. I had projected my own control onto others and blamed them. I had become a judge or persecutor to avoid playing the victim. This was a very important step for my healing.

You can believe that I owned it and asked for forgiveness and strength to be more accepting of others and to be able to own my own negative traits. Learning to love ourselves involves the acceptance of our dark side. And in my case, I was raised with the belief system that we control our external circumstances to get what we want and to prove we are right. The problem was that it didn't work in relationships. I was forced to look inward and let go of my genetic patterning and face myself. It wasn't easy, but it was worth it. My relationships with my children transformed, as did all my relationships.

It is all part of the fodder for growth. We all have blind spots. We can see others much more clearly than we can see ourselves.

Where are you hiding? What are other people close to you saying about you? Are you listening? Are you willing to see one iota of truth in what they are saying? If you are, you can transcend the darkness within yourself and your life will take on new meaning. You will have peace, respect, and love surrounding you. I am living proof!

A Note About Change

Resistance from others is always to be expected. Very often those closest to you will scoff and mock you in your attempts to be honest. Don't despair. Stay at it, realizing that no one likes change! But as we continue to work on ourselves, we will heal emotionally, mentally, spiritually and physically and our relationships will begin to reflect that change. Stick with it! Perseverance will be needed to heal. Keep telling yourself you are worth it! In time, your loved ones will see that it is real and start honoring your efforts.

Galatians 6:9 - NIV

And let us not grow weary of doing good, for in due season we will reap, if we do not give up.

Case Studies As Examples

(All cases are fictional and are for the purpose of example only)

CASE STUDY #1 – MEET MARY

Mary is a homemaker raising 3 children. She loves her husband and children and does everything for them. Mary works day and night to take care of raising the kids. She keeps a clean house. She goes to church on Sunday and makes sure to volunteer in church activities monthly. She washes and starches her husband's dress shirts because he likes it the way Mom used to do it. She creates all organic meals for the family, because she wants them to be healthy, but she snacks all day on chips and fast food, because she is so busy driving kids to school and cleaning house and doing laundry and running errands, that she can't find the time for herself to eat healthy. When her husband comes home, she has his dinner prepared, but she resents that he doesn't see how much she works on his behalf. She hears her mother's voice, "It's always better to give than to receive". She tries so hard to be kind to her husband and to her kids, but every now and then Mary breaks down and runs to her room feeling unappreciated and unloved, and ends up with a migraine. She works tirelessly and seems to get nothing in return. She gives and gives and gives, but she finds herself 30lbs overweight, wearing the same clothes every week (the kids and husband need new clothes more than she does, and besides she wants to lose weight before she buys new) and her hair is beginning to go gray. She can tell her husband doesn't find her attractive anymore, and their sex life is almost non-existent. Because of her neediness, she pours herself into her children to find love. Mary decides she can't take the migraines anymore and needs to find answers from God.

Here are some answers Mary might receive based on doing the AAA program with an open heart that wants answers through prayer.

Phase I: AWARENESS FOR MARY

Where has my focus been?

Mary, your focus has been on others and not yourself. You are not being selfish, but you lack boundaries. It would do you good to find some boundaries so that you are not giving yourself up completely and then resenting it.

Who am I being? (Victim, Judge, Rescuer)

True, you are being a servant, but is it out of true love or codependence? When you aren't honest about your true feelings, and you are serving others and not taking care of yourself, you are being a people pleaser.

Mary examines her inner negative dialogue to separate feelings from fact and to find the truth:

Mary's Victim: Mary's inner dialogue goes like this: "My husband and children don't see how much I do for them. No one shows me love and I show them love all the time. I give and give and give and get nothing in return."

    a. Is it truth? Yes and no. Mary has the power to change all this by being honest with those she loves and taking back her power instead of giving it away. She has trained them that she is only supposed to give and not receive. The responsibility is hers.

Mary's Judge: Mary's inner dialogue goes like this: "They don't deserve all my love. They are selfish and I am not. I am so angry inside, and they are giving me a migraine."

    b. Is it truth? No. She loves her family, which is why she wants to serve them. She doesn't love herself! The migraines are from her struggle within herself to be loved, and from deep seated, unexpressed anger and resentment.

Mary's Rescuer: Mary's inner dialogue goes like this: "My family would fall apart if I wasn't here to take care of everything. They are too busy to accomplish these things without me. I am supposed to serve their every need if I am a good wife and mother."

   c. **Is it truth?** No. All families can adjust to new routines, new behaviors with each other, and new levels of respect when they are discussed. No one is indispensable. Divorces and family battles happen all the time, even when people think they are doing the right thing.

What is my belief system around this issue? (Is there an old belief system that is ready to be acknowledged and changed?)

As soon as Mary asked for angelic assistance, she heard her mother's voice in her head telling her "Mary, it is more blessed to give than to receive." She remembered how pressured she felt to always be the perfect, giving little girl. Mary realizes that her mother taught Mary how to martyr herself, teaching her the extreme of the truth that it is more blessed to give than to receive. Mary realized her Mom did the same thing in the family, and had set a pattern for Mary. She began martyring herself, acting out of this distorted truth, rather than from unconditional love.

Mary has now heard the truth. She has become aware of the roles she has been playing and what is behind it.

Where are you unaware? Are you ready to open your heart to receive the truth before God? If so, you will begin to understand that you are no longer a victim of your illness, your circumstances, and others. Go for it! Be vulnerable! God already knows who you are and what you need. Call on God the Father, Mother and Son to hear your prayer and open your heart to truth. THEN FACE IT! Mary did it, and so can YOU. Mary's next step is PHASE 2: AWAKENING.

PHASE 2: AWAKENING FOR MARY

Mary has just been given the truth from God within her. She now must ask herself the big question, **"Am I ready to surrender to change?"**

It is now her decision to feel it deeply within (even the negative emotion of it) and take full responsibility for her actions. She must go beyond her pride and surrender herself naked before God. Emotions play a huge part here, as we must go into the negative feelings of what who we have been being to get to the truth of our misalignment. It isn't comfortable, but it is necessary for healing. This is where Mary can either fall back into her negative pattern of blaming others or muster up enough courage to face herself deeply and ask God to help her change.

AWAKENING is the point of agreement with God about what we are really doing. Only when we are in the place of fully accepting our mistakes can we be cleansed of them. This is the point where we can either enliven our DNA and upgrade it or leave it in a disempowered, fallen human state. The process may take a little time, but the longer we sit in the pain, the worse it feels. The answer is going into the pain and facing it. The sooner you go through it, the faster you go into the light and peace. Choose to make a decision to awaken your Divine DNA in that moment and don't give the darkness an opportunity to steal the truth from you by planting negative thoughts in your mind! You are now in the spiritual battleground. Your decision at this point determines your action steps.

When Mary asked herself if this was truth, she remembered Jesus' words in her mind.

Matt 9:13 - NIV

But go and learn what this means: 'I desire mercy, not sacrifice.' For I have not come to call the righteous, but sinners."

As bad as it felt, Mary knew it was the truth. She admitted to herself that giving herself up was her own doing. She knew her husband and family loved her, and she wasn't being honest with them about how she felt. She decided she didn't want to play the victim, the judge or the rescuer any longer. She wanted to be honest with herself. She wanted to change her inner life so her outer life could change. She believed that she could have a life that included love for herself and boundaries. She told herself that it was o.k., and that she was ready to let go of the negative thoughts and belief systems that were no longer working for her. Mary's tears were real, which is often the case when we realize and accept responsibility for the games we have played. The Bible calls it repentance. Mary surrendered to God's truth. Now she must take action.

Where have you been unwilling to face the truth? Awakening means taking full responsibility for everything in our lives. If we truly see others and our surroundings as a mirror image of what we are doing, it makes sense. We can change our outer surroundings by being aware of and awakening to the truth that we create it all! Now you have a choice to move it out of your life. This is where it gets exciting!

Let's see how Mary does it.

PHASE 3: ACTION FOR MARY

In Mary's case, here is what it might have looked like:

Anoint yourself with Christian Healing Oils*

Mary selected Gold, Frankincense and Myrrh, recognizing her initiation and commitment with God to change. Then she added Oils of Courage in order to be able to speak her truth in love to her family. Then she added Oils of Solomon for wisdom and protection.

Pray a Prayer of Confession

Mary selected a prayer on Loving Herself and speaking her truth. See Chapter on Specific Prayers you can use and adapt, or just pray to Father God from your heart.

Ask God what Action you need to take to create this new way of being.

Mary asked of God and was given a number of answers.

a) Mary could talk to her husband about her realization that she has become over-caring and over-serving, being careful not to blame him in any way, and asking for his support to find balance for herself.

b. She can begin to create a regimen for herself that includes a 20 minute prayer, and meditation time before anyone gets up in the morning. She can anoint herself with Christian Healing Oils and ask God to help her love herself, and heal her imbalance daily.

c) Mary must be diligent about her thoughts and emotions. She needs to let all negative thoughts and emotions pass through her without sticking! It's like she can allow them to operate without focusing on them. She can redirect or CONSCIOUSLY FOCUS her thoughts to a higher truth and her emotions will follow. If she waits for her emotions to change, she will be stuck and go back down the black hole of self-pity and hopelessness. Sometimes declarations can help. I AM LOVED. I AM POWERFUL. IT IS LOVE TO HOLD BOUNDARIES FOR MYSELF. I AM NOT BEING SELFISH BY HOLDING BOUNDARIES.

d) She can begin to take steps toward loving herself. She can watch her diet, and lose weight. She can begin doing something with her hair and clothes that fit within the family budget and make her feel more beautiful.

e) Mary needs to visualize herself being healed, and feeling happy and loved. When she can continue to see herself this way, she will retrain the mind to create it.

The bottom line is Mary needs to work on her own God-esteem (the truth of who she is), and learn what it feels like for God to love her unconditionally. Then she will be ready to truly love others in a way that honors HERSELF as well as her family.

As Mary puts this into practice, within 21 days she will begin to see change in her external environment with her family.

What happens when Mary meets resistance?

Resistance from others is always to be expected. No one likes change! But as Mary continues to take care of her own healing, her emotional life will be uplifted. She will feel happier and will create better health for herself. Her husband and family will begin to see the changes in Mary, and will respond accordingly. They only want her happy! It is all within Mary's power, as she finds happiness in balanced service. Mary must be willing to trust God for the outcome.

What about you? Are you willing to suffer through the resistance in order to find peace and well-being? It is a necessary step for us all in order to reach our goal of health.

CASE STUDY #2 – MEET JOHN

John was just diagnosed with Type 2 Diabetes. His doctor says if he doesn't change his life he will die. He is 50 lbs. overweight, and works as a mechanical engineer at a computer 6 days a week, 10-12 hours a day. By the time he gets home, the rest of the family has eaten, so he stops and grabs a burger and fries and soft drink or other fast food most nights. When he was growing up, he and his Mom ate fast food a lot, as a reward for an achievement. Dad wasn't around because he was always working. That was ok, because Dad gave John nice things. This was the way his parents rewarded him.

John's wife has begged him to stop working so hard, seeing the stress in his face, knowing he has high blood pressure and high cholesterol on top of it all. She has been trying to give him supplements and ways he can bring down his blood pressure and cholesterol and shows him articles on diet and its effects on his conditions, but he turns a deaf ear. She also sees their family falling apart, because their teenagers don't have Dad home most of the time. She is angry with John and is ready to leave him and take the boys.

It is time for John to ask himself some serious questions. John is at a critical place. If he faces this, it could save his life. If he doesn't, he risks losing his wife and kids and ultimately his health even to a point of death. While he has been in distinct denial, if John is willing to go deep and do the work, he can expect miraculous results.

Self-honesty is one of the biggest parts of awareness. Our minds can tell us that what we are doing is alright because it has been acceptable in our lives for so many years. What needs to happen is a willingness to surrender to God, pray with a heart to know the truth.

If John is willing to go into his heart and call on God, he might hear something like the story I have created in the following pages.

PHASE I: AWARENESS FOR JOHN

Where has John's focus been?

> John's focus has been on himself. Sure, he brings home the bacon, but he has never shared himself through his heart and his time. Is he being selfish? Yes. And it has become self-destructive and ended up as a medical illness. Obviously, John has been focused on his job. He is being a mechanical engineer, allowing that to define

who he is. Why? He spends time there because he gets something from it. He receives accolades for being a good engineer on his job. His ego gets stroked. He also makes good money. It is really more about the ego though, because he has plenty of money now after all these years, and doesn't have to work the hours he works.

John, your focus has been entirely on yourself. You are being selfish and not listening or being concerned about others.

Who is John being? (Victim, Judge, Rescuer)

John is being a left-brained, logical man who has not opened himself up to God, even though he calls himself a Christian, attending church weekly. His heart and emotions have not been a part of his life. He is focused entirely on serving his own desires and ego. John has made his work his life, instead of having a balanced existence that includes his wife and family. The only joy he gets is from his job. He has forgotten how to relate to people and has buried himself in his computer. It's easier when he doesn't have to communicate, and he does as he pleases to indulge his food cravings.

John's Victim: John's inner dialogue goes like this: "My wife and kids don't understand how hard I work to put food on the table. They don't appreciate me at all. I pay all the bills, they live in a gorgeous home and have luxury cars, and they don't understand that all that is because of me.

a. **Is it truth?** No. John is closing himself off to the family and doing what strokes his ego. He must open to considering what others feel and what his part of the problem is, rather than blaming others.

God created you to be in harmony with your relationships and environment by understanding that they are your greatest gift. If you want to heal, you must begin listening to others and seeing that their messages are from God.

John's Judge: John's inner dialogue goes like this: "They don't deserve all that I give them. If she wants to leave, she can leave. Then those selfish teenage brats can find out how hard it is to earn a living on their own. I work so hard, I deserve to eat what I want and I don't need anyone telling me differently. Besides, I don't think it will make a difference. Doctors are idiots. I'm not going to die."

a. Is it truth? Yes and No. John is playing God again. He thinks they can't go on without him and is gambling that the money he provides will keep them from leaving. Eventually, though, his wife and kids won't be able to continue the way things are and they will leave. John needs to be honest with himself. If he continues to be a tyrant and do what is bad for his body, he will end up without a family and it will cost him his life eventually.

John's Rescuer: John's inner dialogue goes like this: "It's time for me to take care of me, and it's ok that I don't want to change. My family would fall apart if I wasn't here to take care of everything. I need to take care of myself in a way that makes me happy. I deserve it."

a. Is it truth? No. John has every right to make a decision to hurt himself. But really, what victory is there in self-abuse and self-sabotage? What he is saying is he can die if he wants to. This is true. But why would he want to?

This type of thinking is not rational before God.

What is John's belief system? Is there a hidden belief system that is underlying John's behavior?

John has several distorted belief systems. First, he believes it is ok to spend 90% of his time away from his family and not interact with them. He believes his job as a husband and father stops at providing money. Second, he believes it is ok to reward himself with fast food because he works hard, even though it is killing him. Third, he doesn't believe what the doctors are telling him. He is smarter about his health than they are. John is unwilling to learn new things about himself and his health.

Romans 8:28 - NASB

And we know that all things work together for good to those who love God, to those who are called according to his purpose.

Even though John has almost killed himself because of his denial, he is still being given an opportunity to be cleansed through surrender to God (truth). There is no timeline for healing on God's side. It's just that on our side, the longer we wait, the more the damage we do to our physical bodies and the harder it is to reverse. Remember, God's other universal truth says we reap what we sow!

If and when John is ready to face himself with an open heart, John might hear something like this:

> John, you are playing God. You are in complete denial and are hurting yourself and others because of your unwillingness to listen. You have not surrendered to Me.
>
> John examines his inner negative dialogue to separate feelings from fact and to find the truth:

b. **What is my belief system around this issue? (Is there an old belief system that is ready to be acknowledged and changed?)**

> As soon as John asked for angelic assistance, he got a picture in his mind of him and his mother at a fast food restaurant where he was being honored with food for getting good grades in school. He realized that his Mom had done this to reward him, but he had somehow connected his goodness and appreciation from people with eating fast food. It was a big revelation for John! He wondered if he would be or could be healthier if he changed how he felt about rewarding himself with food. He realized that would help. His wife was trying

to show him but didn't know how. He realized he was the one who needed to change.

John then asked if there were other mind patterns that needed changing. He closed his eyes and listened, after anointing himself with Oils of Courage. He got another picture in his mind of being alone as a child, wondering why his Dad didn't love him enough to spend time with him. He instantly was able to see how he had created that same pattern with his kids his father had with him. He had made his work the place that gave him rewards, but he had ignored his children.

John felt horrible. He felt he had failed his family. So now he has the big step of self-forgiveness and taking action to change.

With this manual in hand, John went to the next step... AWAKENING.

PHASE 2: AWAKENING FOR JOHN

John asked himself the big question, **"Am I ready to surrender to change?"**

There is a lot to be surrendered here. His angels and guides are opening him to truth he hasn't been willing to face in 40 years. As he opened his Bible and asked for help, he was led to the following verse:

John 8:31-32 - NIV

So Jesus said to the Jews who had believed him, "If you abide in my word, you are truly my disciples, [32] and you will know the truth, and the truth will set you free."

John realized how much he had strayed from his spiritual path. He asked Jesus to assist him to live in truth, and to be humble and begin to hear His voice. John sobbed deeply. Jesus heard the call and came to his side with other angels who assisted in John's healing. They gave John assistance energetically, and John stopped sobbing and asked for forgiveness. He was forgiven in an instant.

After what seemed endless agony, John became a new man. He was in his heart. He had connected to the divinity within himself, and something inside him had changed. He knew now the action he must take.

PHASE 3: ACTION

John anointed himself with Christian Healing Oils on his 3rd eye, palms, bottoms of his feet and on his heart. He was clear that he needed to clear his energy centers from his crown to his feet. He selected the following:

Holy Oils of Anointing (3rd Eye)

Oil of Solomon (Palms)

Oils of Courage (Heart)

Oil of Magdalene (Feet)

Three Kings (neck)

John Prayed. He confessed his denial of God. He confessed his need for God. Then he prayed according to his written list so he didn't get lost. As he is praying, he is visualizing the energy coming into his body from the top of his head to the bottom of his feet. He is using his imagination to see rays of light that are coming in to heal him, and noting their colors, texture, taste and feel. John prays for the following healing from God:

a. Healing of my mind to see the truth
b. Healing of my heart to love myself, my wife and my kids
c. Healing of my physical body
d. Healing of my speech so I can show love
e. Healing of my habits with food
f. Healing of my emotions that need constant reassurance

John Asked God what action steps to take.

John asked of God and was given a number of answers:

a. John could ask for a spiritual coach or seek a pastor that he can meet with once a week to hold him accountable for change in a positive way.
b. John could go to his wife and share his revelations about himself and ask her forgiveness for his stubbornness and resistance to her love.

c. John could ask forgiveness of his children for not being there.

d. John could set an intention to change his work habits so that he is home at reasonable hours, in time for dinner together with his family.

e. John could set up a meditation with God daily, so that he can stay out of denial and in his higher God DNA.

f. He could begin to change his diet and eating habits, asking God for clearing of the damage he has done to his body.

g. He could make an appointment with the doctor to put him on a plan that will be conducive to healing his diabetes.

h. John could set up a new reward system for himself that includes doing something fun without junk food! He can share it with his wife so they can agree on the rewards (i.e., going to the movies or play golf, or whatever)

3) What happens if John fails?

We all fail in our attempts to change, but we only fail in the minute we fail! Each minute, hour, day offers new opportunity. We are powerless, and can't change ourselves with only our own strength. John needs to remember to surrender to God daily, and take one day at a time. He could make a journal of his progress so he has a marker that he is really doing it. When he fails, he can have a system for starting over the next day correctly!

1 Peter 5:8- 9 - NIV

Be alert and of sober mind. Your enemy the devil prowls around like a roaring lion looking for someone to devour. 9Resist him, standing firm in the faith, because you know that the family of believers throughout the world is undergoing the same kind of sufferings.

Negative Entities and Dark Spirits

Jesus addresses very adamantly that there are demons and entities that work against us. He cleared them from people, addressed them by name, and healed people from their possession by them. It must be understood that these entities are real, and are operating at all times. Christian Churches call it "the devil" but in my experience with healing, there are basically 2 categories:

1) Negative Entities – Human beings who have died and have not gone to the light. They need light in order to stay in spirit form, so they attach to living beings to suck their energy. Some of them don't mean harm. Sometimes they are simply loved ones who are confused and don't want to leave. Sometimes they are purposely attached to suck from you.

2) Dark Spirits – Demons and Fallen Angels. These are beings that have never incarnated as humans. They are angels who followed Lucifer. The Demons are their henchmen, created by Lucifer with no connection to their hearts or God. They only serve the darkness. This was the primary reason for Lucifer's expulsion from Heaven. He was playing God.

There is a difference between negative habits and patterns and negative entities and dark spirits. However, when we consistently repeat mistakes and don't turn to God for forgiveness, we create a portal of entry for all negative beings. They can go within our spinal columns, organs, central nervous systems, brains, and blood. They can be all pervasive.

All people are subject to attachment and oppression by these entities and spirits. Don't worry! You can be attached and oppressed and not possessed by them. There is a difference. Do know, however, that you are better off getting them cleared because they are detrimental to your thinking and creating joy. They delight in robbing our joy and work hard to create destructive tendencies within us that leave us feeling separate from God.

If you are concerned about this, feel free to contact me at info@christianhealingoils.com. I have a network of healers who specialize in this type of work. They are fierce warriors of light who work with guides and angels from beyond the veil to clear these disturbances. They can name the type and organ or structure of attachment. They can also provide protection from future invasion.

Don't think you are above it! We all have had entities and dark spirits. Many times, physical illness is one of the results of infiltration and attachment.

You are not bad and wrong. You are love and light. That is truth. We all carry ancestral fear within our DNA, along with all the negative thought and emotional patterns that go with the histories of our lineage. By investigating and healing it, it may save your life!

A word of warning. Don't seek to clear entities on your own. They won't go by command of their host. It takes spiritual forces of light that are beyond this realm to clear them. A knowledgeable spiritual healer or pastor can assist you in this type of clearing. Work first on changing your habits and patterns. If you still sense you are being oppressed, contact me and I can arrange a healing.

Christian Healing Oils™

GOLD FRANKINCENSE & MYRRH were the gifts (frequencies) of the Magi given to Jesus for his initiation into mastery. Gold brings wealth, happiness and comfort. Frankincense & Myrrh were used for purification and healing. They were more expensive than gold. www.christianhealingoils.com

Christian Healing Oils™

THREE KINGS has the essences of Sandalwood, Myrrh, Juniper, Frankincense, and Spruce with Almond Oil. This blend opens the subconscious mind through pineal stimulation. It releases deep seated trauma. It is grounding and spiritually uplifting at the same time. Brings inner peace and tranquility; it is a vehicle for increased psychic awareness and spiritual enlightenment. www.christianhealingoils.com

Christian Healing Oils™

OILS OF COURAGE contains the essences of Rosewood, Blue Tansy, Frankincense and Almond Oil. This blend was used by Roman soldiers before battle. It has the emotional impact of stimulating courage. Adds confidence, purpose, serenity, communication and self-awareness. www.christianhealingoils.com

Christian Healing Oils™

OILS OF GLADNESS Hebrew 1:9 This blend contains Frankincense, Myrrh, Clary Sage, Ylang Ylang, Litsea with Almond Oil. These essences impact the emotional centers of the brain and affect a positive and uplifting feeling. Increases psychic ability and the capacity for inspiration, learning skills and discipline. www.christianhealingoils.com

Christian Healing Oils™

ROSE OF SHARON Song of Solomon 2:1 This is Cistus the Desert Rock Rose. It heals the wounded heart and opens one up to new emotional experiences. It was used by the ancients to heal wounds, regenerate cells and boost the immune system. www.christianhealingoils.com

Christian Healing Oils™

OIL OF SOLOMON Exodus 3:30-34 Frankincense, Myrrh, Galbanum, Cistus and Damascus Rose with Almond Oil imparts wisdom and leadership to the wearer. Solomon used it to connect to the spirit world. It connects the root and crown chakras clearing and aligning all chakras and assists the rise of Kundalini energy (Ascension/Rapture). www. christianhealingoils.com

Christian Healing Oils™

HOLY ANOINTING OIL of Moses Exodus 30:23-24. God gives Moses and all generations to follow a recipe for anointing oil. It includes: Myrrh, Cassia, Cinnamon, Calamus and First Olive Oil. This is the oil given to Aaron and his caste of apothecaries to purify the Temple and the congregation. Jesus sent this oil with his disciples to heal the sick. www.christianhealingoils.com

Christian Healing Oils™

OIL OF THE MAGDALENE blends Spikenard, Myrrh, and organic almond oil. This is the blend used by Mary Magdalene on the feet of Jesus before the crucifixion. It alleviates pain, fear, and anxiety. It can be used for deep meditation. www. christianhealingoils.com

Anointing Locations

In Chinese Medicine, each organ contains an emotion. To understand where you need to anoint, you should be able to identify the negative stuck emotion or mental construct that needs to be cleared in the process. Here is a chart that may help you. (compliments of Gooing Chiropractic)

1) Governing Vessel (GV-20) – Brain. The Master Meridian associated with all functions of body all the way from top of the head to the bottom of the spine. Associated with cerebrospinal fluid, immune system and mental functions.

2) C1 & C2 –Brain and Central Nervous System.
   C1 - Blood Supply the Head, Bones Of The Face, Brain Inner And Middle Ear, Ears, Eyes, Pituitary Gland, Scalp, Sympathetic Nervous System
   C2 - Auditory Nerves, Eyes, Forehead, Heart, Mastoid Bones, Optic Nerves, Sinuses, Tongue Hypothalamus – Gland that links the CNS to the endocrine system via the pituitary gland. Controls the body's emotional response system.

3) Pituitary – Produces many hormones needed for the body to regulate temperature, urine, thyroid, etc.

4) Deep Sleep Point

5) Brain 2 – Emotions and Stress

6) Brain 3 – Emotions and Addictions

7) Occipital – Vision problems

8) Conception Vessel – Connected to life force (thymus). Connected to the Yin (female) meridian. Cell Energy Point

9) Kidneys – Associated with fear and cleansing of blood.

10) Pericardium – The surrounding sac of the heart. Associated with loving feelings and joy or lack of same. Links sexual energy with heart.

11) Parathyroid Glands – Associated with unexpressed anger and rage.

12) Lung – Grief and Sadness

13) Thyroid – Depression & Anxiety

14) Thymus/Heart – Links emotions with reason. Trouble can indicate an inability to balance the two.

15) Liver – Associated with anger and rage.

16) Gallbladder – Unexpressed anger that results in bitterness.

17) Stomach – Things that are indigestible

18) Pancreas – Love – Not getting enough

19) Spleen – Worry & foreboding.

20) Anterior Sacral – Negative Emotions related to Pleasure

21) Small Intestine – Digestive troubles

22) Large Intestine – Usually associated with holding on too tightly to thoughts and processes of life. Can be associated with shame and disgust. Is also connected

to the Lung Meridian, where sadness and grief can be connected.

23) Bladder & Urinary Tract – The bladder is linked to social relationship conflicts, to external communication, as well as to territorial conflicts and socialization.

24) Prostate/Uterus – Feeling useless.

25) Pubic Bone – Feeling undervalued.

26) Circulation – Stagnation

27) Lymphatic – feeling a need to defend oneself, to justify oneself, in order not to feel undervalued

28) Kidney – Deep seated fear. Can be Ancestral. Fight, Fear, Shock.

29) Adrenal – Adrenal depletion is the act of not accepting what is. Fight or Flight.

30) Posterior Sacrum – Tensions associated with who I am

36) Quadriceps & Hamstrings – Fear of moving forward

38) Gluteus Maximus – Something in life is literally a pain in the butt!

Organic Meridian Acupuncture Reflex Points

3 Hypothalamus
4 Pituitary
Eye
Brain (GV-20) **1**
Eye
Parotid Gland
Parathyroid Glands **11**

12 Lung (LU-1)
15 Liver (LIV-14)
16 Gallbladder (GB-24)
18 Pancreas (LIV-13)
R only

Thyroid **13**
Thymus
Heart **14**
Stomach (CV-12) **17**
Spleen (LIV-13) **19**
L only

Navel
21 Small Intestine (CV-4)
23 Testes/Ovaries
24 Urinary/Bladder (outflow)
26 Pubic Bone

Anterior **20**
Sacral CC (CC-3)
22
Large Intestine (ST-25)
Testes/Ovaries **23**
Prostate/Uterus **25**

27 Circulation

28 Limphatic
(outside little toe)

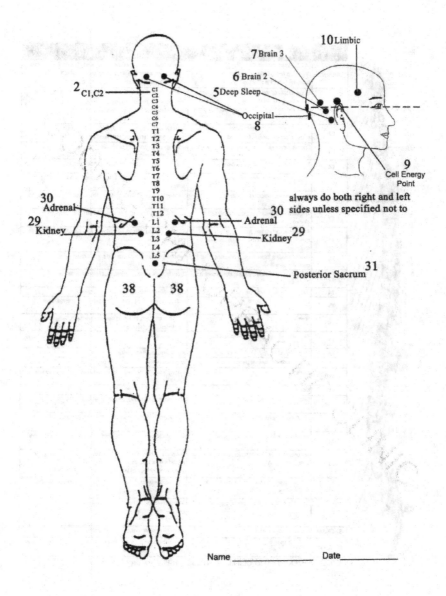

10 Limbic

7 Brain 3

6 Brain 2

5 Deep Sleep

2 C1,C2

Occipital

8

9
Cell Energy
Point

C1
C2
C3
C4
C5
C6
C7
T1
T2
T3
T4
T5
T6
T7
T8
T9
T10
T11
T12
L1
L2
L3
L4
L5

always do both right and left
sides unless specified not to

30
Adrenal

29
Kidney

30
Adrenal

29
Kidney

Posterior Sacrum **31**

38   38

Name _____   Date_____

Name _____   Date _____

VERTEBRAE	Areas & Parts of the Body	Possible Symtoms
BRAIN	GV20, Hypothalamus, Deep Sleep, Brain 2, Brain 3, Cell Energy, Limbic, Occipital Lobe, Parathyroid	Anxiety, Brain Fog, nervousness, insomnia, head colds, nervous breakdowns, amnesia, sleeping sickness, chronic tiredness, allergies, Immune / Auto Immune Reaction
C1	Blood supply to the head, the pituitary gland, the scalp, bones of the face, the brain itself, inner and middle ear, the sympathetic nervous system	Headaches, high blood pressure, migraine headaches, mental conditions, dizziness or vertigo, Stress Reaction, Biofilms, Heavy Metal Toxicity, Radiation Toxicity
C2	Eyes, optic nerve, auditory nerve, sinuses, mastoid bones, tongue, forehead	Sinus trouble, crossed eyes, deafness, eye troubles, earache, fainting spells, certain cases of blindness
C3	Cheeks, outer ear, face bones, teeth, trifacial nerve	Neuralgia, neuritis, acne or pimples, eczema, Neurodegeneration
C4	Nose, lips, mouth, eustachian tube	Hay fever, catarrh, hard of hearing, adenoids
C5	Vocal cords, neck glands, pharynx	Laryngitis, hoarseness, throat conditions like a sore throat or quinsy
C6	Neck muscles, shoulders, tonsils	Stiff neck, pain in upper arm, tonsillitis, whooping cough, croop
C7	Thyroid gland, bursae in the shoulders, the elbows	Bursitis, colds, thyroid conditions, goiter
T1	Arms from the elbows down, including the hands, wrists and fingers, also the esophagus and trachea	Asthma, cough, difficult breathing, shortness of breath, pain in the lower arms and hands
T2	Heart including its valves and covering, also coronary arteries	Functional heart conditions and certain chest pains
T3	Lungs, bronchial tubes, pleura, chest, breast, nipples	Bronchitis, pleurisy, pneumonia, congestion, influenza
T4	Gall bladder and common duct	Gall bladder conditions, jaundice, shingles
T5	Liver, solar plexus, blood	Liver conditions, fever, low blood pressure, anemia, poor circulation, arthritis
T6	Stomach	Stomach troubles, including nervous stomach, indigestion, heartburn, dyspepsia, etc.
T7	Pancreas, islands of Langerhans, duodenum	Diabetes, ulcers, gastritis
T8	Spleen, diaphragm	Hiccoughs, lowered resistance
T9	Adrenals or supra-renal glands	Allergies, hives
T10	Kidneys	Kidney troubles, hardening of the arteries, chronic tiredness, nephritis, pyelitis
T11	Kidneys, ureters	Skin conditions like acne, pimples, eczema, or boils
T12	Small intestines, fallopian tubes	Rheumatism, gas pains, certain types of sterility
L1	Large intestines or colon, inguinal rings	Constipation, colitis, dysentery, diarrhea, ruptures or hernias
L2	Appendix, abdomen, upper leg, cecum	Appendicitis, cramps, difficult breathing, acidosis, varicose veins
L3	Sex organs, ovaries or testicles, uterus, bladder, knee, circulation	Bladder troubles, menstrual troubles like painful or irregular periods, miscarriages, bed wetting, impotency, change of life symptoms, many knee pains
L4	Prostate gland, muscles of the lower back, sciatic nerve	Sciatica, lumbago, difficult, painful, or too frequent urination, backache
L5	Lower legs, ankles, feet, toes, arches, lymph	Poor circulation in the legs, swollen ankles, weak ankles and arches, cool feet, weakness in the legs, leg cramps
SACRUM	Hip Bones, buttocks, Pubic Bone	Sacro-ialic conditions, spinal curvatures
COCCYX	Rectum, anus	Hemorrhoids or piles, pruritis or itching, pain at the end of spine on sitting

GOOING CHIROPRACTIC CLINIC (714) 556-9188 www.drgooing.com

Sacred Prayers

The prayers here are designed to assist you in going into your own heart. They are written from my heart and stated as I would be talking directly to God. The best kinds of prayers are those from your own heart! They are real. God isn't concerned with the words you use. He is concerned with your state of being (heart). The sample prayers simply give you a way to know how to pray.

Note that these prayers invoke all 3 parts of the Holy Trinity; Father, Son & Holy Spirit. I use Mother God as the Feminine Aspect (Holy Spirit). Use what is most comfortable for you. There is no right and wrong in prayer. God hears your heart.

Primarily, though, we are praying to the Father/Mother God, in the name of Jesus.

General Healing Prayer (Truth)

Suggested Oils: Holy Anointing Oils
Forehead between the Eyes (Third Eye)
Palms and Bottoms of Feet

Father in Heaven and within my heart, lean in to hear my request.

Archangels, Enlightened Masters and Ancestral Guides of Light, draw near, hear me, protect me, and comfort me.

I have fallen short, yet know that through Jesus, all things can be made pure and whole.

Restore me to my original Divine Blueprint without stain or mark.

Feed my soul with pure manna from Heaven, your Divine Love and sustenance.

Restore me to my Godliness.

Clear me of my injustices, my fear and negative emotions, and guide and direct my path.

My body is giving way to my own negative choices in life. I am guilty of _____.

Show me the truth of my crooked road. Show me a better way. Fill me with healing light and love.

Heal me now I pray, in Jesus Name.

<u>Self-Forgiveness (Grace)</u>

Suggested Oils: Oil of The Magdalene, Anointing Oils,
Three Kings
Palms, Third Eye, Bottoms of Feet, Kidneys

Mother/Father God, I need your tender mercy and strength.

My limbs are numb from my own mistakes. My soul is weary.

Create in me a clean heart. Help me to lean on you rather than stay in my mind and its worldly games of power and control.

Connect me to my higher awareness, and let me feel deeply the pain I have inflicted on myself and on others. I am aware of it. I acknowledge what I have created.

I am ready to change my ways. I am ready to consider others as being connected with me. What I do to my brother or sister, I do to myself.

Forgive me also for not responding when you tried to show me truth.

Forgive me for becoming stiff necked at your lessons.

Heal me from my pride.

Heal me from my anger.

Heal me from my fear.

If you are with me, no one can be against me.

I trust in the Lord with all my heart, and forsake the way of the world. Show me the way.

Abba, Father. Amma, Mother.

Let me heal from my mind, will and emotions. Let me feel whole in your presence and love.

In Jesus Name, Amen.

<u>Forgiveness of Others (Surrender)</u>

Suggested Oils: Rose of Sharon, Three
Kings, Gold, Frankincense & Myrrh
Palms, Third Eye, Bottoms of Feet, Tops of Feet, Throat, Heart

Heavenly Father/Mother,

My heart is broken within me. I am carrying anger/bitterness/resentment for my spouse/brother/sister/friend/coworker/child.

They have caused me great pain and I can't let it go.

What is it within me that created this? Help me to see.

What is it within them that wanted this situation? Help me to understand.

Help me to accept all responsibility for my part.

Help me to forgive them for their part, in the same measure as I forgive myself.

Set me on the wings of the Eagle, so that I may soar above the circumstances of this situation.

Let me fly high with a new perspective through your eyes.

Let me be like Christ when he forgave the thief on the cross.

Let me clear my body, mind, and heart of all desire to return the pain and suffering.

Help me to see he/she who has hurt me as something within me that needed to be addressed.

Let me clear myself, and leave their choices between them and You.

Help me to truly forgive, and let go of all retribution, anxiety, worry and sorrow.

In Jesus Name I pray, Amen.

<u>Betrayal (Courage)</u>

Suggested Oils: Oils of Courage and Three Kings
Back of Neck, Third Eye, Behind Knees,
Palms, Bottom of Feet, Kidneys, Heart

Mother/Father God, I am at my lowest point.

Please surround me with protection from my Angels, Guides and Masters who are working with me.

Those whom I trusted have betrayed me. It feels like they were never my friend, yet I know we are connected for a reason.

Help me to perceive this betrayal as a needed lesson from you. Help me not to lash out in anger and return pain for pain.

I feel like I am in Gethsemane. I feel like I have been crucified. I share in the sufferings of Christ and therefore in His Grace.

Help me to let go of all the anger and rage and resentment I feel now. I know if it will stick in my body and keep me sick if I hang on to it, but I don't know how to let it go.

So I confess that I can't do it by myself. Help me, O Lord, to release the pain.

Help me to trust in you.

Help me to believe that you are my rear guard, and I have nothing to fear.

My limbs are weak and my heart barely beats.

Thank you for this lesson. Help me to understand it in the days to come. Help me to forgive my brother/sister so that I can move forward in love.

Give me strength and peace in my hour of need.

In Jesus Name, Amen.

<u>Negative Emotions (Hopelessness, Anger, Fear, Rage, Intolerance, Pride, Selfishness)</u>

Suggested Oils: Oils of Courage, Oils of the Magdalene,
Three Kings
Third Eye, Back of Neck, Ears, Kidneys,
Palms, Bottoms of Feet

Divine Mother,

I am drowning in my own emotions. Save me!

Help me to let go of projecting my negative emotions on others. Help me to release the negative energy within me so that I can me clear and focused on love.

Create in me a clean heart, as you bring awareness of the thoughts that are creating these emotions within me.

Are they ancestral patterns? If so, let me heal from the transgressions of my lineage.

Are they my own creation in habits and patterns? If so, show me where I am blind to what I am doing.

Restore to me the righteousness of God. I AM HOLY. Let me feel HOLY.

Raise my vibration to a state of joy. Help me to let go of my judgments and preconceptions of my own reality.

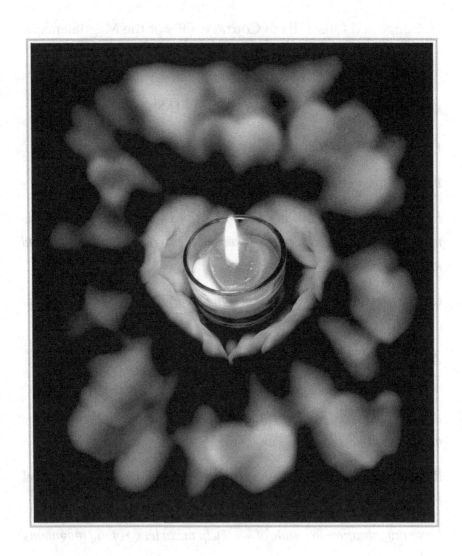

Help me to breathe deeply and receive the Holy Spirit through breath.

Let all negative entities and dark spirits be cast out of my body and field. Help me to understand where to go to get help if they are controlling me.

Create in me a clean heart.

Whisper the truth in my ears, and soothe my thoughts.

Help me to feel the joy and comfort and nurture of your love.

Wash me in the purity of the divine emanations of water.

Purify me with the fire of the masculine.

Set me on heights to restore my soul to love.

In Jesus Name, Amen.

Physical Illness (Disease)

Suggested Oils: Holy Anointing Oil on 3rd crown; Three
Kings on 3rd Eye; Oils of Courage on neck and spine; Rose of
Sharon on Brain 2 & 3; Oil of Solomon on navel and coccyx;
Oil of the Magdalene on palms and soles of feet. You can also
place any of these oils on specific organs that need healing.

Dear Father/Mother God,

*I am suffering in my physical body. I call in the Angels, Guides &
Masters to create a double diamond tetrahedron of white light around
me with mirrors facing inward to magnify and intensify my healing. I
pray that they will bring forth illumination of my mind to understand
the reason I am ill.*

I ask for understanding for the cause of my dis-ease and its remedy.

Why am I sick?

Is it unto death?

Am I glorifying you as I undergo this trauma?

Create in me the desire to manifest good health.

*Create in me the ability to utilize the elements of air, fire, water, earth
and ethers to alchemize whatever needs to be re-created in my life.*

Show me the negative emotions that created this dis-ease.

Show me the mental belief systems that need to be changed.

Free me from the bonds of my own emotional/psychological prison.

Free me from the belief that I need something physical to heal me.

All I need is YOU.

Fill me now, in the hour of my need.

Heal my body. Heal my mind. Heal my emotions. Heal my spirit.

Create in me a clean heart.

Let me be a shining example of love.

In Jesus Name, Amen.

Restoring Balance (As Above, So Below; As Within, So Without)

Suggested Oils: Oil of Gladness on Brain 2 and Brain 3; Rose of Sharon on throat; Gold, Frankincense & Myrrh on crown and feet; Holy Anointing Oil on 3rd Eye; Oils of Courage on Solar Plexus and Kidneys

Father/Mother God,

I see where my life is out of balance.

I see where I am leading with my (masculine) (feminine) side and have neglected balance in my life.

I want to balance my life.

I want to honor my relationships so that all people feel loved and cherished by me.

I want to balance my time so that my values are in alignment with what is truly important.

Help me to understand who I have been being, and where I need to change.

Help to have the courage to consciously choose a new way of aligning my values and balancing my life.

Help me to consider my loved ones most important.

Help me to understand that my work must be balanced with my spiritual life; my mind with my heart, masculine with my feminine, my human and physical with my spiritual.

Help me to be a learner again.

Help me to let go of all things I thought were important and choose fresh.

Help me to experiment and create an adventure out of life.

Help me to live in the present, rather than in the past or the future.

Create in me a clean and balanced life.

In Jesus Name, Amen.

Addiction (Self Control)

Suggested Oils: Holy Anointing Oil on Crown and 3rd Eye; Rose of Sharon on Heart; Oil of Solomon on throat and solar plexus; Oils of Courage on back of heart and temples; Three Kings on palms and feet

Father God,

I call in the Archangels and Masters of Light who work with me.

I am aware that I am helpless in my addiction.

I know that you have the power to heal all things, and that it is me who keeps falling into old habits and patterns of escapism.

My heart is wounded.

My thoughts are impure.

Create in me the will to create a clean and holy life.

Create in me the ability to see myself as I truly am…. Loved, connected and accepted just as I AM.

Help me to feel the truth of who I AM.

Create in me a clean heart.

Bind in me all forces who are working against my healing.

Remove from my life all people who take me down and tempt me.

You always provide an escape. Give me that escape now in dramatic ways.

I love you, Lord God. In you I place my trust.

Help me to bend to your will.

In Jesus Name, Amen.

MAIL-IN COUPON FOR FREE OIL

We want to send you a free sample!

Clip this coupon and mail to:

Christian Healing Oils Sample
c/o World Leaders Alliance
3225 McLeod Dr. #100
Las Vegas, NV 89121

Your Name:_____

Address:_____

City,State,
Zip_____

Email_____

Phone_____